In the Worshipful Company of Skinners

In The Worshipful
Company of Skinners
Endre Farkas

The Muses' Company Series Editor: Catherine Hunter
Cover design by Terry Gallagher/Doowah Design Inc.
Author photo by Yassaman Ameri
Printed and bound in Canada

We acknowledge the financial support of the Manitoba Arts Council and The Canada Council for the Arts for our publishing program.

Canadian Cataloguing in Publication Data

Farkas, Endre, 1948–
         In the worshipful company of skinners/Endre Farkas.
Poems.
ISBN 0-920486-51-7

I. Title.
PS8561.A72I5 2003   C811'.54   C2003-903951-1

J. Gordon Shillingford Publishing
P.O. Box 86, RPO Corydon Avenue, Winnipeg, MB Canada R3M 3S3

Dedicated to Jean Steinbruck whose birch-bark journal first set me on this journey and to Henry de Lotbinière Harwood whose pride and passion for Canada inspired me to quest after the true nature of this *quelques arpents de neige.*

Table of Contents

The Company Rules

Procure a trusty Savage,
See you safe to his country that
We have not as yet had any traffiic with.

Be sure to converse with the guide
As much as possible so you may
Attain his language and his hides.

Tell them you love the Savages.
Make them presents. By your presence
Exhort them to come to you.

Persuade them not to war against another
But to be at peace so that they may hunt
And bring their skins to trade for goods.

Use them civilly. Give each some trinket
And lead them down the ensuing year
With many such glittering promises.

By no means use force. Use guile
Yet do not be afraid of a firm hand
And above all be upon your guard.

It is not likely but The Runners of the Woods
In hearing of you being amongst the Savages
May way lay you.

Take care to make the Savages your friends.
By this friendship, you may be able to head
Them against the said Runners of the Woods.

But otherwise do not offer or let them molest
The said Runners of the Woods,
Unless they are the first transgressors.

Upon the contrary side,
The French, knowing of your coming,
May come to see you as a friend.

If so, use them kindly but upon no account
Go with them and keep at a fair distance
For you cannot be too careful.

Be wary of their fondling, artful
And knowing disposition toward deception.
Keep your own counsel.

Having a compass, pen and hand lined paper,
Be very exacting in keeping a journal
Of your travels and daily observations.

Mention the day, the month and year.
Observe the soil as you proceed: trees, herbs,
Also take particular notice of minerals.

Remark the place and situation where you find such.
When by water, observe the course:
Try the depths; know how many miles you go.

Mark down everything that occurs to your view
Mention when you come to any river or lake
Or prairie or mountain and the season.

Take every observation and remark to you
Whether it be fair or foul and
Be it ever so trifling as you may imagine.

Enter the names of every creature tame and wild,
Of every White Canadian, Bois Brulé and Savage
So that we may all take advantage of them.

And lastly, for your own preservation
Take particular notice of all these instructions
That you may not fail in the performance thereof.

And you may depend upon it. For any loyal service
You may do by such a journey across this country
The Company will sufficiently reward you.

Today

Today,
As I have mastered my numbers and letters,
And entered my manhood of the thirteenth year,
I am ready to enter the service of my betters
And with honest toil toward my fortune steer.

Today,
After much effort, petition and patience,
My dear father has me apprenticed
To those masters of our great nation
Whose might around the globe, is feared.

Today,
Dear friends, with whom games of tag and chase
I played among the giant walking stones of Brodgar
And hide-and-go seek in the chambered cairns
Of my beloved Orkney Isles, I now leave you for afar.

Today,
Is the time of tearful embraces, kisses
And blessings. And with little money
And only my Bible as my true compass,
I set sail upon the Stygian Sea.

Today,
Into Ultima Thule
I disappear.

At Sea

Dear God
This sea is endless. Land has fallen off
The face of the world. It has been swallowed
By the Stoor Worm's watery mouth.

I am so frightened.
I feel so alone, so far from the hearth,
From my dear parents and my Isle;
For ever, I fear.

The sleeping quarters are dank and cramped.
My blanket is the stagnant, rank air.
In my hammock I sway and loll
Above the vomit, the rats and their droppings.

The sailors are crude and foul smelling,
Their skins and speech are tanned by their salty life
And yet, though weather beaten and harshly treated,
They are cheerful and often sing songs while at work.

And though I am from an isle oft battered by the sea
And have spent time upon the waves,
Still, when a storm overtakes us
They make sure I am to rope securely tied.

The captain, liking my countenance,
Has in a masterly fashion taken me under his wing
And has begun to instruct me in the reading of charts.
In the guidance of the heavens and the ways of men at sea:

In the red sky of night
The sailors delight,
But in the red sky of morning
They see storm warnings.

Dear God
The sea is endless and I am sick for shore.
I am in limbo, between home and hell
Oh hear my prayers and have mercy
Upon my body and my soul.

Still at Sea

At sea, wonders never cease.
Water is the bottomless road upon which we sail
Waves are endless frothy flames licking at our floating home.
Vastness is the pure and salty air we inhale.

At sea, wonders never cease.
The sky is the eternal canvas
Upon which the changing weather paints
Our fortunes fair and foul.

It is our beautiful and ominous heaven,
Our constant holy dome
To which we send our prayers
And look to for signs.

At sea, wonders never cease.
Creatures on the wing swim in air
And from grace dive for other creatures
That leap from the deep and slice the air.

At sea, wonders never cease.
Days and nights I spend at its mercy
I breathe its awe, and fear
Its gentle breathing.

Land

Land first appears as a mirage
Something hoped for, for so long
So absent that the vision is not to be trusted
Even when shouted from the crow's nest.

Land crops from the sea
As the shoots of prayers I have planted
In the liquid soil which we
Have ploughed these past weeks.

Land emerges from the sea
Like the green tongue of the monster
On whose stormy back for nigh
Forever we've been tossed.

Land swims out to meet us
Like a firm handshake
To welcome and draw us
Into its rocky-firm bosom.

Land! I am in my natural element.
And though it is an alien place
I am sure of my steps again
And have a settled stomach.

Land not unlike my own beloved Isle,
Which the sun first blesses, which the heavens
Keep watch over, and which the sea embraces
Like a shimmering diamond necklace.

Land, that upon first night
Blankets me in memories and longing
Becomes the battlefield of the Borealis
Upon which gods' blades spark these brilliant flames.

God I give thanks for deliverance
And ask Thee to abide with me
In my new endless wilderness
In this New found land.

Here

Here
I traverse rivers and lakes the size of seas,
Woods as webbed as nightmares,
Prairies endless as their skies
And mountains as savage as the heathen gods
Who there do dwell.

Here
Away from the Old World,
In an older world that is new to me,
I am to hunt unnamed beasts;
Fur-rich creatures, which crawl, swim and slither.

Here
To this eternal white wilderness
To this brief green glory where
The mighty antlered Pegasus bellows
And roams in herds that carpet the land;
To teach me trading skills and to test my faith
The Company and God's will have sent me.

Here
The wilderness is master, its vastness
Makes sane men mad,
Savages to see spirits
And I, to fear the ways to wealth.

Here
In this world Old and New,
Underneath these stars uncountable,
Brilliant as African diamonds,
I, as Adam in the Garden of Plenty, swear
As I am servant now
I will one day master be.

It is for this I have come
It is for this I am here.

Apprenticeship

I willingly submit my life to He
Of the Company who will teach to me
The secret Arts and Crafts to prosper
In these hostile lands.

I to heathen woods will go,
Where no sunlight shines, and dwell
Unnamed beasts that whole devour men.

I will, if need be inspire the frozen air
That flesh and spirit claws and rends
And face blasts that batter sight and amputate touch
And wade in quicksand snow that would
Suck me down to its God forsaken hell.

I will walk and walk and walk
Among blood-sucking insects
Gladly backpack ninety pound lessons
Across the sharp canines of this land
Until the body's blisters are well learned.

I will subsist my seven apprentice years
Even if destitute of family and food
To prove my fortitude and Faith.

I will learn from my masters well:
Bear the upside the head, the boot in the rear
And the curses of my betters so that one day
I may, like a real Company Man,
Likewise command and teach.

The Savages

In the evening
They wave me to their smudge fire
And apply strange salves that soothe.

In them I feel the forests,
The lakes and the seasons.

If only they were not such Heathens.

The White Canadians

The White Canadians
Are descendants of the first French settlers
And are the most thoughtless
And the most improvident race in the world.

The White Canadians
Are like children. All finery
They set their eyes upon they must have,
Even at exorbitant Company prices,
Even for their Savage wives.

The White Canadians,
What with buying horses
Gambling, drinking and indulging
In the sins of the flesh, no wonder
Their wages quickly vanish.

The White Canadians
We engage to harvest stones,
To chink the palisades, to mud
The stores, to cut wood
To prepare the garden, to trim
The dogs for the travois, and
To make new whiskey kegs.

The White Canadians
On our voyages commence at daybreak
And from thence to night-fall
Occupy their time with back-bending paddling
And portaging our goods.

The White Canadians
Soften the severity of their labour
With songs, displaying the elasticity
Of spirit that so distinguished
Their vivacious ancestors.

The White Canadians,
Are good natured and affectionate
Each other call, related or not,
Mon frère or mon oncle.

The White Canadians,
Of them this must be also said:
No other people are capable
Of enduring so much hardship.

God Bless them.

Runners of the Woods

My Master says,
These Runners of the Woods were,
When they did own this land,
Brought here by French law,
Which insisted more upon quantity
Than quality.

They were brought for marriage
To women of their station,
For cultivating farms and family,
But soon tramped off into the woods
To hunt the deer, to spear the salmon,
And to lay traps for any animal
With fur on its back. And often
Took Savage wives.

My Master says,
These *Coureurs de Bois*
Do not so much civilize the Savages
As the Savages barbarize them.

And their ranks are reinforced by Half-Breeds
And Savages who, for whatever purpose,
Are dissatisfied with steady work.

My Master says,
He has not yet found one honest man among them.
They are generally scoundrels and a nuisance.

My Master says,
These Runners of the Woods
Are now a part of Our Majesty's booty.
And when not employed by The Company,
Are called Freemen.

We are much plagued by these Freemen.

The Guides

The Savages
Are chiefly used as guides,
Canoe men and hunters,
And their squaws as warm winter robes.

The Savages
Are quarrelsome and vengeful
Insubordinate and sullen
Indolent and fickle
Cowardly and treacherous.

The Savages
Are immoderately attached to ardent spirits
And during their intoxication
To check their ferocious propensities
The utmost firmness is necessary.

The Savages
Are brought up to religion by The Black Robes
And sing hymns more often than paddling songs.
But these hypocritical wretches,
As soon as they start to sing God's praises,
We more carefully observe their actions
And double the watch.

Voyageurs

The old voyageurs from the young
Who have never passed this way,
Expect the treat of a drink, and
Those who refuse
They most hardily baptize.

To the men of my canoe I give
Spirits which make them merry and
Help them to forget with what heavy hearts
And weeping eyes they departed
From their dear children and wives.

Coming to difficult rapids
Where many have drowned,
For the bodies found or not
They remove their hats,
Make the sign and say a short prayer.

They, who are in the habit of
Voyaging this way
Say their prayers and erect crosses here
More often than at home.

At one I counted no less than thirty.

With such dismal sights
Almost continually before our eyes
We press forward with ardour,
The rashness of youth and
The hopes of good fortune.

In this country
So it has always been
And so shall forever be.

Amen.

The Forest Fort

By long sawn pickets twenty feet high,
Two and a half feet broad and six inches thick
For protection as well as trade
The Fort is surrounded.

On top for ramparts and loop holes
A range of smooth balustrades four feet high
Stands against Savages scaling the walls.

A strong gallery five feet broad all around extends
And at each corner a large water reservoir,
Two hundred gallons as security against the element
In the schemes of Savages we most dread.

Inside are storehouses,
Dwellings for the hands,
And in front of these, of sawn timber
With port holes and slip doors,
Another twelve-foot wall.

Thus should the Savages get in
They will see on all sides
Nothing but a wall before them
And beside these outer gates
Which open and shut by pulleys
Two double doors the entrance secure.

We have four pieces of ordnance,
Ten wall pieces,
Twenty boarding pikes,
Sixty muskets and bayonets,
A box of hand grenades,
And a small mortar above the gate.

We trade through a secured iron door in which
There is an opening of eighteen inches square.

The Savages are never admitted,
Save on important occasions
And only by our consent
Can they have intercourse with us.

Thus we are safe in our Gibraltar.

Tricks of the Trade

My Master says,
When The Chief arrives
The honour of waiting on him
Falls to the master.

In a servile capacity
Go forth to meet him
And know, the further you go,
The greater the compliment.

Invite him in, see him seated
And, if required, untie his shoes
And dry his socks.

Hand him water
And listen with grave attention
To all he has to say on Indian topics.

Show him you value his information
Give him some trinkets
Sometimes even articles of worth.

My Master says,
When you light the *calumet* of peace
Direct your face first to the east
Then to the other cardinal points
And give each a solemn puff.

Hand the pipe to The Chief
Who will do the same
And will pass it to his right hand man
And so on until the pipe is smoked out.

Then The Chief, with ceremony,
Will produce his own
And the others their own.
Now, The Chief will solemnly declare
That he is a long time very hungry for a smoke.

At this time present The Chief
With tobacco *ad libitum*.
The more pipes in circulation
The greater the compliment.

My Master says,
The grand point of this ceremony
Is to know how far one should go,
Because by overdoing it
One may endless troubles invite

At this time
The trading may commence.

My Master says,
Observe as they throw down the produce of their hunt
And squat themselves around it in a circle.
Each will divide his skins into different lots and
For one he will want a gun
For one ammunition
For one a copper kettle
For one an axe or a blanket or a tomahawk or a knife.
And finally, for one, ornaments for his wife.

They are shrewd and hard dealers
Not a whit inferior to us Scots.

After the first round
Beginning always with The Chief
Give them each
Half a gill of Indian liquor.

Into it The Chief will dip a finger,
Let a few drops fall on the ground,
Offer a few drops to the above,
The rest he will drink without delay.

Each chief has his own rite
But after that gets drunk
As fast as possible.

Thus will you drink and trade
Until about midnight when
They fall into liquored dreams
On the bare ground and snore
Contentedly till late next day.

My Master says,
Always be the first to rise
And start the rites of business
While the Savages still struggle
To find their feet and clear their drunken heads.

Know these things, and heed these words:
A trade is good when you get what you want
And make the customer thank you for it.

The Beaver

The Beaver is the bigness of a water-spaniel.
Its fur is chestnut or black and always soft.

It has two lays of hair,
One long and shiny, grainy as a man's.
The other fine and silken as a lady's.

The Beaver does not hibernate
But with great and intricate elaboration
Adapts to seasonal changes.

It builds circular lodges, twenty feet across and
Three to five feet high and cements them with mud.

The lodges have two entrances above water,
One, two-feet wide as a runway
One, ten-feet long for supplies.

The Beaver, in winter feeds on birch and poplar,
Willow, cottonwood and the bark & twigs of hardwoods.
In summer, chiefly on the roots of plants.

The Beaver weighs between thirty to sixty pounds.
Its meat, though fatty and oily, is agreeable.

The tail is a delicacy,
And the White Canadians, being Catholic,
On Fridays Christen it a fish.

It is a stationary animal,
Slow at best and therefore
It can be attacked in all seasons.

The Beaver is on The Company's Coat of Arms
Whose motto is *Pro Pelle Cutem*

This the men translate as
By any means we'll skin you.

Raison d'Être

The Maxims of Power
The Mysteries of Theology
The Labyrinth of Justice and
The Secrets of the Healing Arts
Are vested in furs that robe
Emperors and Popes and
Lawyers and Physicians.

The quality of fur upon one's head,
Around a mistress' shoulders,
Confers as much as lineage;
Ranks Kings above cabbages,
Priests above Physicians and
Lawyers above the Law.

It is well known that furs cure
Head aches and rheumatism,
Stomach distemper and gout;
The ailments which defeat
The healer's most potent herbs,
Leeches and blood letting.

And our skins,
In mad hatter's hands
Can bring most favourable judgements
From the magistrates of fine society.

And even the common folk,
Who once traded the misery
And penury of their earthly life
For the promise of ease in Heaven,
Now see the fashion of their betters
And demand while on earth
Felt hats and fur coats.

So it is
For The Emperor's empire
The Priest's piety
The Gentleman's hat
The Lady's stole and
The servant's dream
We brave the Western Main.

So to this land that God gave to Cain,
Which the Frenchies call
Quelques arpents de neige
And the poets and philosophers
The Savage Garden,
We sail as the loyal servants of
The Worshipful Company of Skinners.

The Company Men

We are humble loyal traffikers
Using the strictest trading principles
Teaching the Savages our Christian ways.

We are traders, explorers and dreamers
Serving our coppery customers our spirits,
Beads, blankets and other desired articles.

We are The Company's eyes, ears and feet
Engaged daily with these wily innocents
Who look to us for guidance.

We, whose calloused hands
Hold more often pelts and guns
Than pens, keep immaculate ledgers.

We are the compass points
Charting the shapeless north
In search of fur-clad gold.

We are the true Company men
And note that we have passed
And shall forever pass this way.

Rock Eggs

I fear we have very few days left to us.

We are twelve in the deep winter woods
And for the last fifteen days have subsisted
On what is sufficient for two.

It is the season of long sleep and absence.
Game has gone and an unholy emptiness prowls.

These last three days of winter darkness
Hunger reigns as we have only dried cherries and tallow.

We are obliged by a gnawing necessity
To subsist on what the Savages call *As-se-ne Wa-quon-nek*
And the White Canadians call *Tripe de rocher.*

It is a moss that adheres to the dark side
Of rocks like a growth to an illness.

We scrape it with our fading strength and boil it
Into a greenish-brown glutinous substance.

Surprisingly, is very palatable.

The Gift

We have nothing, not even our will.

Each lies with his last thoughts
And commends his soul to God.

The trees speak and the bushes part.

They have come to us
And offer us beaver tails.

After our meal I ask what they want for them.

When our chief sends us to trade
He always sends something as a gift.

I thank God for delivering us.

Perchance

Perchance, for honest toil,
I will rise to Clerk, Trader, Factor;
And finally, God willing, a Wintering Partner.

Perchance, for sending back the finest pelts,
My own commodious apartment have
With ante-chambers, a mess-room and closets,
And an Indian Hall and glorious ballrooms
And bedrooms with glass windows.

Perchance, for keeping accurate accounts,
Become proud chieftain for The Company,
One who with a firm and just and Christian hand
His allotted lands, posts, lakes, forests
And Savages command.

Perchance, for shrewd trading,
Ramble at my pleasure;
Enjoy my morning ride, my fishing rod,
My gun, my dog, my hunt.

Perchance, for loyal service,
With other like-minded masters
In Montreal, in grand splendour, yearly gather
To discuss weighty matters, and to God,
King, and Us raise full and profitable tankards.

Perchance, for all this,
Tomorrow and tomorrow the promise to be
A part of the strong, free and wealthy Bourgeoisie.

The Bourgeois Children

The Bourgeois are remarkable
For indulging their children.
Instead of teaching them industry and frugality,
They let them run about at will.

They think they are doing their sons a favour
And forget the hard-gained lessons
And how they served them well
In their own advance.

From the Savages and Freemen
These Bourgeois children learn every vice:
Race horses, dogs, shoot arrows and get drunk
But will not degrade themselves with honest labour.

They know nothing, want to know nothing
Do nothing and can do nothing
And look at us who work
And are disgusted.

This is all very well,
While their fathers are in service
But when they leave The Company,
So must the lazy, ignorant children.

And when their fathers are scarcely cold
In their graves, the sons lay their hands
Upon their fathers' hard-gained wealth
And the last shilling is soon gone.

So, lost and penniless in the friendless city
They return to the country again
Like returning geese,
To the land of their nativity.

But here too they are strangers
And again they try their bows and arrows
But have forgotten even that Savage skill
And are lost.

The Half-Breeds

The Half-Breeds who
The White Canadians call *Bois Brûlés*,
Burnt Wood, due to their complexion,
Are good canoe men and on foot or on horseback
Excellent hunters.

Daring, passionate, and brave,
They possess all the vivacity of their fathers
But manifest their mothers' Savage ferocity
Especially when insulting allusions
Are made about their mixed origins.

As they grow up, they resemble
In almost every respect the pure Savage
But are more designing, more daring,
More dissolute, more indolent,
More thoughtless and more improvident.

They are unrestrained in their desires,
Sullen in disposition, proud in carriage,
Fond of flattery and associate with
White Canadians and Savages
And acquire all the bad qualities of both.

The Dogs

We purchase them from the Savages for a trifle.
They are generally of the wolf breed.
The young we train and sell back to them
For twice the price of a horse.

In summer the Half-Breeds
Keep them starved and penned,
But after dark let them loose, and they become
The terror of the camp.

In wet weather the dogs make the camp
A kennel and the stench is intolerable.
The Savages and the Half-Breeds
Seem impervious to the foul air.

They, along with the White Canadians,
Eat dog and say it is as palatable
As a young pig and much the same flavour.
Only the direst of necessity could make me eat it.

Their women might go without their blankets
Their daughters without their beads
But the husbands must have their dogs
And the dogs their scarlet ribbons and bells.

These dogs are vigorous and long-winded.
For them a hundred miles a day is not uncommon.
I have seen two such dogs draw a sledge
Of five hundred pounds twenty miles in five hours.

In this country where the snow is very deep
They sink but a little. And for a short distance,
Besides provisions for themselves, can
Draw more than a thousand pounds.

I know not any Savage, Half-Breed or White Canadian
Upon whose shoulders such a burden is placed
Who can render half the service.

The Buffalo

The Buffalo has a narrow, short face.
From eye to eye the brow is two palms across.

Its eyes stick out at the side so that
When running, it can see what is pursuing it.

When it runs it throws its head back, yet
Its goat-long beard still drags on the ground.

Around the middle of its body it has what appears to be
A girdle. In front of it, the hair is very long and rough
Like a lion's. But behind it, it is very fine and wooly
Like a lamb's.

It has a hairy great hump larger than a camel's
And it is regal when it charges.

Its horns are short and thick,
Not much above the hair,
But are still to be avoided.

Its tail is short and almost hairless
But at the end there is a clump
And when it runs it carries it erect as a scorpion.

In summer, often, as far as the eye can see,
Commencing at every point of the compass,
The ground is covered with their one formed body.

The plain becomes a single black and hairy sea of motion
And when Nature strikes a flint and the plains are aflame,
We watch the buffalo, their hair singed off,
Eyes swollen and closed fast, lose their nobility
Smash into boulders and tumble down cliffs into creeks.

In spring when the river is clear of ice
We go down to the risen banks
To watch the drowned, three to five deep, float by.

And for sport, to the other side and back,
From carcass to carcass, we walk.

The Savage Language

No matter which,
It's all gibberish,
Most unpleasant to a Christian ear.

From their mouths
Clucks and twitters, sighs and grunts
Fly faster than startled pheasants.

With their arms, hands and fingers
Stab, slash, punch, flow, accent their jabber
And cleave the air.

All transactions: legal, business and
Social are preceeded and followed by
Endless invocations and thanking of the Spirits.

Their village names are unspeakable
Their directions go on forever
And destinations are measured in stories and moons.

They have no writing to speak of.
And all they have to read is the sky,
The lakes, the creatures and the land.

The Hunters

These Plain Indians are excellent horsemen,
And during the buffalo hunt their skills
Are displayed to the fullest.

Without hesitation and at full speed,
Over the roughest ground they ride
Into the midst of the massive herd
Which surge in wild confusion.

They overtake a beast,
And just before abreast of it
Discharge an arrow high into its back,
Between the hip and small ribs.

Their intent is to sink the arrow
Full and straight into its heart
So its effect is more marked
And the presence of the shaft will show
To whom belongs that most delicious and
Boastful trophy of the tongue.

The Gift from The Great Mystery

For the Savages
The hunt is a different business.

From its hide they make
Teepees
Robes
Saddles
Shields
Shirts
Gloves
Moccasins
Ropes
Leggings
Quivers
Par-fleche sacks.

From its sinew
Bow strings
Twine
Thread.

From its bones
Shovels
Arrows
Axe heads
Scrapers
Traps
Runners for sleds.

From its throat, heart sacks and paunch
Pouches.

From its brain, liver and fat
Tanning grease.

From the rough skin of its tongue
Hair brushes

From its horns
Spoons
Cups
Powder horns
Arrowheads.

From its marrow
Soup.

From its hooves
Rattles
Glue.

From its tail
Scabbards for war clubs
Medicine rattles.

From its excrement
Fuel.

And from its skull
The sacred totem for the next hunt.

The Prairie Fort

Pleasantly situated in a deep valley
We have planted a large, compact fort
With many good buildings,
Palisades and bastions.

The soil being good, we grow
Large crops of potatoes and grain.
But Spring and Fall frosts are injurious to wheat
And seldom does it come to maturity.

Adjoining the fields is a fine,
Level ground of two miles
Which allows for horse racing,
The chief amusement of the summer season.

With the Half-Breed Freemen and Woods Indians,
The Cree and Assiniboine, we trade individually
Or in small groups. The Plains Tribes: The Blackfoot,
Sarcee and Blood require more ceremony and security.

We are well located, well defended
And on the whole, with these warlike people,
A peaceful and profitable trade is carried on.

Lazy Savages

All day on every hill we see them.
They think and talk of nothing
But horse racing, gambling and war,
And when tired of these
Idleness is their delight.
They spend their lives like women
At their toilet, paper looking-glass
In one hand, paint brush in the other.

Fifty at a time they come,
Interrupt us at our busy work,
Rap at the gate and call out
I want to trade.
But when you attend,
They have nothing to sell
And laugh in your face.

My master has resolved,
No matter how urgent their call,
He won't answer until
Twice he has walked backwards
And forwards across the fort
After which nothing surprises or ruffles his temper.

In their own estimation
They are the greatest people.
They look at us who labour
And from the bottom of their hearts
Despise us and call us slaves.

Strong Medicine

My master assembled the chiefs,
Showed them a small bottle
And spoke most eloquently:

Although we are weak in number
We are strong in medicine
And if you attack us
I will open the bottle
And send it among you.
If we are not attacked or robbed
It will not be uncorked.

The Chief of the chiefs
Listened most solemnly
And replied most wisely:

If it is let out it will run like fire
Among the good as well as the bad.
We are friendly to you whites
And will remain so.

The Chiefs spoke no more
Their stoic countenance
Well recalled their people's
Aching pains and prostrations,
The pustules and scabs
The bleeding and the blindness,
And the raging fever before death
That enwrapped them like a blanket.

They greatly dread my master,
His great power in the small bottle.

The chiefs honour my master
And in solemn ceremony name him
Great Chief Small Pox.

The Savage Race

Today
Ominous clouds.

An adventurous Cree
Appears on foot
Followed by keen Blackfoot
Who have come for sport
For torture and for scalp.

Today
Heavy rain begins.

I wish to save the Cree but fear
The Blackfoot who are armed
And already in the stockade.

Needing peace for trade
I trade for peace
And arrive at a compromise.

We will keep the Cree
Until the next full moon
When they will return for him
And he will be given a sporting chance:
A race of Blackfoot braves against the Cree.

After much talk and smoking
The Chief agrees.

Today
I put the Cree into hard training;
Twice a day for an hour around
The fort at full speed.

He is fed fresh buffalo meat
And is forbidden whiskey.

Each night and morning
He prays in his own way.

Today
Humid.

The full moon has come round again
And with it the Blackfoot.
After much talk and smoke
We secure their horses within the walls,
And, except for knives, take their arms.
And agree to the rules of the race.

They will chase the Cree
But only on foot and only with knives
And to be fair, will give him a start
Of a hundred yards.

The word is given
And with frantic yells
Away the hunters dart.

Within the fort, there is much shouting
And much betting.

The Blackfoot gain quickly
For terror paralyzes the Cree
And escape seems hopeless.

But suddenly,
The very same terror that rooted him,
Releases him. Like a rabbit he is off,
And soon his training begins to tell.

With ease at every stride
He begins to leave them
And after a mile he is far ahead

And filled with confidence
Pulls up for an instant,
Shakes his fist triumphantly
And then is out of sight.

Today
Clear.

All bets are settled.
Trading resumes.

Fire Water

Today Big Arm
In a drinking match,
In a fit of jealousy
Stabbed Auposoi to death.

Auposoi's brother, a boy of ten,
Went to Big Arm's tent,
Fired into his breast
And killed him dead.

Little Shell,
Big Arm's cousin,
Went to Auposoi's mother
And in her tent stabbed her.

Ondainoiache,
Little Shell's friend,
Then went in and
Gave her a second stab.

Little Shell in his turn
Gave her a third blow.
As long as her life lasted
Did they continue to murder her.

This affair kept the Savages from hunting.

Today White Pheasant, drunk,
Fought with his wife, fell in the fire
And was almost roasted but
Still had strength enough to bite off her nose.

He is very ill but I don't suppose he will die.

Today Little Shell that troublesome
Drunken Indian would not let us be,
So in his high wine I put
One hundred and twenty drops of Laudanum.

It had no effect, so by the hair I dragged him.
He tried to stab me with my own knife,
So I broke some ribs and bunged up his eyes so
He could not walk or see or hunt for several days.

To see a house full of drunken Savage men
Women and children is a most unpleasant sight.
They wrangle, upon one another spill rum,
And pull each other by the hair.

They fight most promiscuously
Until at last they fall to the floor
And vomit on each other
What they have just drunk.

The babies on their mothers' backs
Bawl, while the older ones grab at
Their parents' garments and howl
For fear that they might be stabbed.

These shrieks of children form a most unpleasant chorus.

Today just before departure
A large band of Savages engaged in drinking.
To ease myself of one I gave him a dose
Of laudanum in a glass of grog.

It prevented him from further troubling anyone
By setting him asleep forever. This accident caused
A fray in which several men were killed.
So the rest of us had no choice but to fly.

Such accidents and events are the cost of trade.

Today
No extraordinary news
Save of the Act of Parliament
Prohibiting spirituous liquors among the Indians.

This law may ease the trader's life
And bring much needed peace
In this lawless and troubled land.
But it will not enrich him.

Therefore, it is to be ignored.

The Cure

In the morning after drinking
They swarm into the house
For medicine to relieve the effects of liquor.

I make them sit and begin to circle.
I command them to follow me, just with their heads,
but their throbbing pain and dizziness forbids it.

With my back to them I concoct a potion of trash:
Usually of whisky base, raw eggs and any vile colouring
We might have, which I make them smell before tasting

The sharper the application of the concoction,
The greater their faith in its efficacy and
Greater their admiration of me.

They call me The White Medicine Chief
Assume I am all powerful in the knowledge
And the secrets of the Healing Arts.

I assume a solemn countenance.
It is an essential part of the cure.

Their innocence and faith in my powers
I take most seriously.

Voyageurs in Town

Once a year they come out of the woods,
Make up for their dangers and privations
By drinking, rioting, carousing and
Spending all their gains in days.

Once a year in wild forgetfulness,
Settlements become Bedlams
As frantic inmates run to and fro.

Once a year,
When such unfettered characters,
Such motley groups of whisky hunters
Are turned loose at all hours,
In every nook and on every corner,
The decent citizens stay indoors.

Once a year these expert bottle-men
Greet the morning with the tilt of
Unfinished bottles of the night before,
Meet the midday drunk, leaning on
What will not move or spin. And
Supper, they suckle from the bottle.
And by evening are again most skunked.

Once a year these dissolute spendthrifts,
Fearing neither God nor man
Spin out in feasting and debauchery.

And then, penniless, return to the Savages
And the wilderness to hunt,
Until the knife or some other attack,
Dispatches them to their reward.

And though they are unpitied
We have need of them and thank God
That they are as prolific
As the creatures they hunt.

Old Coureurs de Bois

One says
I have been forty-two years in this country
For twenty-four a light canoe man.
No portage was too long for me
And my end of the canoe
Never touched the ground
Until I saw the end of it.

One says
Fifty songs a day were nothing to me
I could paddle and carry and walk and sing
With any man I ever saw.

One says
I had once possessed fifty horses
Six running dogs trimmed in the first style
And had twelve wives in the country.

One says
No Indian Chief had finer horses
No white man better harnessed or swifter dogs
No Bourgeois better dressed wives.

One says
I beat all Indians at the race
And no white man ever passed me in the chase.

One says
Five hundred pounds twice earned
Have passed through my hands
And though I have now not a spare shirt to my back
Nor a penny to purchase one
Yet if I were young again, I would gladly spend all
For another half century in that same-self country.

One says
There is no place else where
A man may enjoy such freedom
As in the Indian country.

To this
All lift their boastful tankards
Bought on credit and in liquored fashion shout
Hurrah pour le pays sauvage!

In saloons
Too old to trade, too poor to retire
These old voyageurs sit around simpering fires and smoke,
Spit, and trade their tall-tale lives for watered-down drinks.

The Ledger

Debit	Investment in goodwill for the Chief	
	Scarlet Coat	1
	Gingham Shirt	1
	Pair of Trousers	1
	Dimity Vest	1
	Braided Hat & Feather	1
	Woolen Hose	1
	Slippers	1
	Silk Negligee	3
	Canton Plates	4
	Iron Bar	1-6 lbs
	Vermilion	1/2 lb
	Flour	10 lbs
	Bread	5 lbs
	Molasses	4 bottles
	Rum	4 bottles
Credit	Skins	
	Beaver	100,031
	Muskrats	51, 033
	Martens	40,440
	Otters	6,143
	Minks	4,328
	Fish	2,268
	Lynx	1,131
	Black Bears	1,591
	Black Bear Cubs	529
	Brown & Grizzly Bears	272
	Cubs	53
	Deer Skins	4,065
	Dressed Original Skins	3,497
	Kitts	2,508
	Wolves	4,502
	Wolves-Damaged	582
	Raccoons	745
	Wolverines	798
	Red and Cross Foxes	1,746
	Caribou Skins-Dressed	173
	Deer Skins-Damaged	906
	Buffalo Robes	1,135

Ledgers do not lie
Debits and credits add up to who we are
And how far we've come in this world.

We are known by our skins
Measured by our canoe loads
And respected for the size of our stores.

There is no great mystery in this
The good deed is the good deal
The worth of a man is his net profit.

Losses and Gains

For debts against skins
For himself and his wife
I equip my hunter with clothing
And the Savages their necessities
And an assortment of small articles gratis:
To the men
>1 scalper
>2 folders
>4 flints
And to the women
>2 awls
>3 needles
>1 seine of net thread
>1 fine steel
>A little vermilion
>$^{1/2}$ fathom of tobacco.

And even if such debts have to be written off
As bad, owing to the debtor's dishonesty,
Disability or death,
I still have what matters most;
A clear profit for the Company.

The Salmon Season

It is salmon season.
The Indians flock in from all quarters
And the quantity taken is immense
Not less than twenty thousand daily
And yet this was not the great fish rendez-vous.

I expected the chief to invite me to supper
And to pass the night in his tent
But we had to pass the night supperless and
Houseless in the open-air camp among
The stinking, rotting fish and snarling dogs.
The night being warm, the stench was terrible.

During one of our fishing days
A sturgeon almost jumped into my canoe
His head struck the gunnel near one of the men
Who instead of taking hold of him
Gave a scream and the fish fell back into the water again.

Tonight my old friend, a Northwester
Was in charge and with his usual kindness
Treated us to a dish of very fine whitefish,
The first of the kind I had ever seen.

The whitefish in the Athabasca is considered
In point of quality, in the same light
As salmon on the Columbia.
And many tall-tale arguments take place
Between those east and those west of the mountains
As to which is best

I give preference to the good old salmon
As the king of all the piscatory tribes.

Harvest

Praise be to God and The Company
We have now in store
Twenty-five thousand salmon,
So each man is allowed four a day.

We have taken
Seven thousand whitefish
Each about four pounds.

We caught a sturgeon of ten feet
Round his middle four feet
And after we took out
Nine gallons of roe and intestines
It weighed three hundred and ninety pounds.

The men have gathered
      1000 bushels of potatoes
      40 bushels of turnips
      25 bushels of carrots
      20 bushels of beets
      20 bushels of parsnips
      10 bushels of cucumbers
      2 bushels of melons
      5 bushels of squashes
      10 bushels of Indian corn
      200 large heads of cabbage

All this beside what has been eaten or gone bad.

Most of the men have their winter wives
Who they call their winter dictionaries;
Women whose warmth and tongues
The men claim serve our purpose well,
As they teach them much about the language,
The ways of its people and the lay of the land.

We are ready for the long season.

Horses

Among the Flatheads, Cortonais and Spokane,
Whose lands are rather thickly wooded,
There are not more horses than sufficient
For their actual use and every colt
On arriving at the proper age
Is broken for the saddle.

But in countries of open plains,
Well watered and thinly wooded,
Inhabited by the Wallah-Whallas, Nez Percés
And Shoshone, thousands roam wild.

I've been told that in Snake Indian country
There are herds varying from three to four thousand.

The Spaniards at San Francisco informed our traders
That, that year, in order to preserve the grass for the buffalo
They were obliged to kill upward of thirty thousand horses.

The Feast

At the centre of the lodge
A sweet fire roasts the harvest
Of the season's hunt.

The squaws run to and fro
In chattering business and delight,
Setting greasy barks and old skins
As plates for delicate viands.

A sturdy Savage,
While preparations are under way,
Guards the entrance with a look
And a war club that keeps the dogs at bay.

The guests sit in a closed ring,
Between their legs hold platters
Filled with the most delicious beaver,
Swan, crane, dog and bear grease
Mingled with roots and berries.

All the nabobs with hungry fingers
Grab large helpings,
Stopping only now and then
To sleek their hair with the grease

The dogs, howling and growling
Behind the banqueting circle,
Pace in anxious expectations.

By him each guest,
For the purpose of self-defense,
Keeps a cudgel.

Yet it happens
Some of the more daring curs
Get out of patience, break through
And carry off their booty but not without
The vengeance of the cudgels.

However, the dogs have their revenge
As the beatings disturb their dormant fleas
Which in turn feast on us. So every creature
From man to dog to flea
Partakes.

The Savages wisely say,
He who does not eat heaps
When he has lots is a fool,
For many moons may pass
Before he has heaps again.

The Savage Faith

They pray to everything:
The sky, the water, the trees
And all creatures big and small;
Even to what they are about to kill.

Their prayers are in the form of songs,
Chants, dances and grotesque masks.
And sometimes the praying goes on for hours
Until they are in a state that is most unChristian.

The elders, men and women,
Who are no longer of any use,
Sit all day, smoke and, to the young ones,
Tell fantastic, pagan tales about their own creation
And what they call the Great Mystery.

They are primitive and stubborn in their beliefs.
Thus must our missionaries, at great personal risk
Wander into the wilderness where their faith
Is sorely tested, and often. Still,
Driven by Christian duty and
With a caring but firm hand
Make them see the light.

Winter Nights

Even if I could
It would afford me little pleasure
To converse with ignorant Canadians.

For conversation all they wish
Are horses, dogs, canoes, women
And tales of strong men who fought the good fight.

Among the Savages the topics are fewer
Limited to the transactions of the day
The number of animals killed
The cunning of the ones that got away
And the oft-retold great battles.

Their taciturnity may be easily understood
If we consider our occasions for speech
The records of history, the pursuits of science,
The systems of politics, and the disquisitions of philosophy.
The transactions of the four corners of the world
Are utterly unknown to them.

I have a few books of hymns and songs
And the latest edition of *Humour*.

I read Darwin's *Botanic Garden*
And the greater part of the *Bible*.

My leisure moments I pass perusing them.
Happily for me I am left alone.

New Year

Today the axe broke.
We have very little food left
And the tent caught on fire.

Today La Brulle's wife
Had a bad dream about her man.
We assured her that her dream could
Certainly come to pass
Which made her decide to leave to find him.

I gave her one arm-length of cloth,
One arm-length of tobacco,
Six measures of powder and 50 balls of shot.

Tonight Bostonais' wife gave birth
To a baby with six toes on each foot
Smaller ears below the others
A man's machinery in front
And a woman's below the kidney.

Today no news.

Trading

Today Chief How How spoke to me.

She is the flower of our tribe
Lovely and fair
Her ochre cheeks are delicate
Her nose-bob, her girdle and her gait
Irresistible.

Her robes surpass in luster her person
Her feathers, bells and her rattles are unique.

I am fond of you and wish
To have my daughter
With the white people.

Today I much thought upon this
And after much talk, examination,
And mature deliberation,
For the good of The Company,
I have decided to accept his offer.

For while I have the daughter
I have the band's friendship, protection and furs.

And I have accepted the custom of the gentlemen
Who remain for any length of time in this savage world,
Rather than live a lonely life, for a wife,
His fourteen-year-old I will take.

Today I gave to Chief How How
Fourteen new guns and blankets,
A keg of rum and dry goods.

After the ceremony
My new father-in-law said

All great men should have many wives
So I wish you to take my second daughter.
One woman is not sufficient for a chief,
Provided they are from the same family.
Observe, I, for my three wives, have three sisters
And I do not lack for love or peace.

I much thought upon this. However,
As I do not have more articles to trade
I must decline.

Ailments

Today
From the original wound of the poisoned arrow
Daoust's shoulder and side are healed up
But still give him much pain and formed an abscess.

I applied poultices of biscuit and water
It burst and he feels much relieved.

Today
Ross can scarcely crawl about
Sick with back and side pain.

With camphorated spirits and warm flannel
I rubbed the parts and it gives him much relief.

Today
Carelessly handling a knife, Desbien
Stabbed a companion near the ankle
And it bled for a long time.

I applied red willow bark
It gives him great relief.

Today
Lafleur is ill with colic
And is in great pain.

I gave him some sweet oil and essence of peppermint
He threw it up so I gave him a dose of jalap
Which he threw up as well.

I then gave him Glauber's salt
Which after a time took its course
But does not relieve him much
In fact his pain has increased.

I gave him an emetic
Which worked well
And he is much relieved.

Today
The Bostonian split his thumb
And because he neglected it
The wound is in a sad condition.

I washed it in sal ammoniac until it bled
Which caused the poor fellow to dance with pain
And to swear he would rather have it cut off.

What I know of the Healing Arts
I have learned from accidents,
From what was done to me,
And from the Savages whose cures
Go with chants and dances
And seem to work more often than our own.

Still
One does well to not get sick.

Moving Day

Today our outfit is ready.
Our summer fort is stripped
And we are ready to trek to our winter home.

Payet, who leads a two-horse cart
Loaded with his private baggage
Boxes, bags and kettles, is our guide.

Next is Madame Payet
With a child on her back
Indian fashion and very merry.

Next is LaPointe his cart loaded
With goods and baggage, belonging to others,
Leads his horses loaded with kettles
Hung on each of their sides.

Next is Madame Bottineau
With a squalling infant on her back
To whom she sings lullabies, to no avail.

Next is Dubé
With his long stem pipe in hand.
His broad-bead-tailed tobacco pouch
Is carried by his Half-Breed wife.

Next is Brisebois
With a fresh lighted pipe in his mouth
And a gun on his shoulder.

Next is Jasmin
With a gun in hand
And a pipe puffing clouds of smoke.

Next is Pouilot
The greatest smoker in the Northwest
Who has nothing but a pipe and pouch.

Next is Livernois
With a young mare loaded with an old worsted bag,
Some squashes, potatoes and a small water keg
And weeds for smoking.

Next is Madame Cameron's mare
Kicking and rearing and snorting
Hauling a travois loaded with bags of flour
Cabbages, turnip, onions and a large kettle of broth.

Next is Langlois
Who is the master of the band
Leading a horse that draws a travois
Nicely covered with a new painted tent
Under which his daughter and Mrs. Cameron
Lie very sick.

Next is Madame Langlois
Following with a slow step
Attending to the wants of her daughter
Who not withstanding her sickness
Can find no other expression of gratitude
But to call her a dog, a fool and a beast.

Next is the rear guard of a long train of
Twenty dogs, some for sleigh and some to eat;
Others of no use except to snarl and destroy the meat.

Today
Over the sun beaten prairie,
Over the flower-flecked rises and dips,
The wagons of a hundred dolorous sounds,
The magpie chattering of the folk.

We roll toward the foothills and beyond
Where the silver threads of rivers wend.
This country has no end.

The Fall Fort

We came upon the Fort,
Was well fortified,
Impregnable
With walls twenty-seven feet in height
With a ravelin and four bastions
With forty mounted cannons

The Savages captured it with ease
And quickly razed it to the ground.

Round about us now
Rusting cannon balls,
Rotting carriages,
Rancid stores.

Remaining is the air of melancholia.
Remaining is the air of departed greatness.

Unwelcome News

Today from Tongue River
From a camp of my Indians
Tented there to make dried provisions,
I received most unwelcome news
From the child of my sister-in-law.

My grandfather chief How How
Went to see if the buffalo were at hand,
He climbed a tree but no sooner reached the top
Than two Sioux discoverers fired.

He had only time to call out
"Save yourselves! The Sioux are killing us!"

He was the first felled,
His body broke the branches as it dropped.

The women and children,
Seeing danger, ran
Through the plains toward an island of woods.

Our four surviving men kept behind us, urged us on
And seeing the war party rushing down upon us,
By brave maneuvers and constant fire prevented them
From closing in on us while we continued to fly.

About two hundred paces from the woods
The enemy did surround and fall upon them.
Three of them fled in different directions
Two were killed but I saw Red Crow escape.

Our War Chief Low Horn remained
To protect us. He waited until the enemy
Came very near, then fired at one who
Appeared to be the chief and shot out his eye.

Some ran into the woods
Where the brush was thick and tangled
But my playmates Gray Back, Deer Runner,
Little Spring and Long Hair were taken prisoners.

My mother, with my sister and I,
Could not run fast enough so she asked my aunt
To carry my sister. When we got near the woods,
With hideous yells and whoops the enemy rushed us.

My frightened aunt threw down my sister
And soon overtook us. My mother seeing this
And hearing my sister's screams
Kissed me and said,

"Take courage my daughter
And try to reach the woods
Go to your elder aunt at the River Post,
She will be kind to you."

She recovered my sister and was running
When by a blow from a war club she was felled
But recovered instantly, drew her knife
And plunged it into the neck of her attacker.

But others coming up dispatched her,
Cut her open, and her heart,
Still quivering, tore out and devoured.
And thus my mother's days ended.

Education

To procure two Indian boys
As desired by our Governor
To be educated at the Red River Colony
I passed the winter in Fathead country.

We have decided,
Because your governor desires it,
To avail ourselves of his boon.

We give you not our servants
Not our slaves to teach
But our own children.

We give you our hearts.
Let them not get sick or die
For if they become sick,
We shall become sick.
For if they die,
We shall die.

Bring them back before they become White
For we wish to see them once more Indian.

Only after many great councils
And after harangues like this
Did The Chiefs agree.

We named
The son of the Kootenais Chief,
After the Governor of The Company,

And the son of the Spokane chief,
After one of the Directors of The Company,

Both were fine promising youths,
About ten or twelve years of age,
And were to be educated at The Missionary School.

Kootenais Pelly at the end of three years,
After making progress in learning, died.

Spokane Gary some years after,
Returned to his own country
With a good English education
And spoke our language fluently.

However, he did not realize the expectations
Entertained of him by his country men,
Nor was he at home in his own home.

Last Will & Testament

I, by free will,
Have come here to seek my fortune
And found a New World that is ancient,
Waters that flow from endless time,
Forests that are thick with mysterious roots
That go to the centre of the earth,
And strange creatures of plenty
That I have feared, hunted, skinned and eaten.

I have come to reason with my senses
To live by feel, to count by breaths,
To travel by songs and pipefuls
And know that The Great Spirit is.

Yet I am still a Christian
And having lived with my Indian woman
As my wife *à la façon de pays*,
As my winter dictionary,
And having had children by her,
I consider myself under moral
If not legal obligation, she willing it
Not to dissolve the connection.

I have taken great pains to instruct her
In the Christian doctrines and duties.
And as long as I remain in this savage world
And if we can live in harmony
My intention is to keep her.

And before I return to my native land
I shall place her under the protection
Of some honest man with whom
She can pass the remainder of her days.

This is my last will & testament.

The Grand Conference

The Company's Great Council Chamber
Is decorated with Indian accoutrements,
With trophies of the trade and of the hunt.

We the Bourgeois, with the eyes
Of our dependents cast upon us,
Consider the whole dignity
As represented in our persons
And conduct ourselves accordingly.

We are the country, the loyal government.
We engage in vast, solemn deliberations,
Hard Scottish reasoning and about the future,
Occasional swells of truthful declamations.

In this grave and weighty council,
Lives are measured in furs
And fortunes in partnerships.
We decide who will and who will not
Become a Bourgeois

In our banqueting hall in Montreal
The tables groan under the weight of
Buffalo tongues, beaver tails, and other luxuries
Prepared by the grand chefs of the city.

And as it is a period of loyal toasts,
Bacchanalian songs and brimming bumpers,
There is no lack of good wine.

We the lords of lakes and forest
Revel in the hall and make the rafters resound
With old English songs in voices cracked
And sharpened by the northern blasts.

Our merriment is echoed and prolonged
By White Canadians and Bois Brûlés,
Who make the welkin ring with French ditties
And feast on what falls from our tables.

God it is good to be rich and powerful.

Civilization

On The Company's advice I left my Indian wife
For Montreal's society so as to enjoy
The pleasures of my wealth
And what comes with it.

News of my arrival among these pale faces
Spread more quickly than smallpox among the Savages,
And invitations to the city's cultured courts
Were as numerous as the latest furs and lacy cuffs.

My Bourgeois bronzed features, Oxford gray hair and
A *dégagé tout ensemble* imparted interest and
Was universally desired. Every night I was wined and
Dined and listened to with breathless attention and
My adventures drew gasps and bravos.

Music and songs followed until the morning hours
When I retired in bewildered joy
Cursing the time that took and barred me for so long
From such civilized diversions.

Marriage

Oh God! Shut out for so many years from
Civilized society, from its many endearments,
I, lord of the forests and the lakes,
Aware of the wily Indian ways
Became the city Savage's easy prey.

My caution and common sense that kept me safe,
That stood me in good stead, that gained me so much
I lost, dazzled as Savages by beads, to pretty prattle.

Too quickly I made my selection
And entered into married life
To an educated female no less
Who becomes legal benedict.

And like a morning after too much fire water,
I discovered that a bright eye, a fair face,
A sweet voice or a tune on the piano
Is rather an empty compensation
For what begins and never ends;
The waste of my hard-earned fortune.

Having spent my years where money is of little use
I find myself disgusted with this place where nothing
Can be had without it and sigh for days gone by.

And if I attempt to remonstrate against her extravagance,
My interesting bronze turns to copper, my Oxford gray
Assumes a vulgar hue. My air *dégagé* degenerates
Into the air slovenly, and an English tongue reminds me
Of all the garrison officers who were dying for her
And all that she has thrown away upon this weather-beaten,
Moss-chewing dog-eating, rheumatic white Savage.

I envy those companions, White Canadians and Bois Brûlés,
Who found when the time originally fixed for quitting
Indian country and wife arrived, they could not
The women who had been, for many years,
Their faithful partners in a moment whistle off.

Children had grown up about them and they could not,
For the moral laws of civilized society,
Shake off their natural affections.

These traders, who by law, could leave their winter wives,
Their temporary unions joined in permanent marriages.
And so on quitting The Company brought their families
Back to Canada, to their purchased estates
On which they now live, Half-Indian, half civilized.

And each night, as the sun sets,
Contentedly sit upon their porches,
In silence stare across their lands,
Watch their progenies abound,
Smoke their calumets in well-earned peace and
At the world's fur-lined, fashionable frivolities
Spit.

Afterword

Ten years ago I came across a fur trader's journal, a beautiful Canadiana artifact, written on twenty-six four-by-eight-inch sheets of birch bark and bound by thread. The title page reads *Journal Pour les Fort des Couteau Jean Commencer le 6 decembre 1802 par Jean Steinbruck Pour N. W. Co.* The volume intrigued me and so began my exploration to find out who Jean Steinbruck was, to discover why his journal was written on birch bark, and to decipher its contents.

One result of this research is the beautiful book *The Yellowknife Journal*, published by Nuage Editions (now known as Signature Editions) of Winnipeg, Manitoba. This book reproduces each of the individual birch bark pages and has, "en face," the transliteration and translation into English by Karen Haughian and Marie-Thérèse Haughian. It also includes an engaging introduction by Harry Duckworth (the well respected fur-trade scholar), recounting Steinbruck's fascinating life. I highly recommend it.

During my journey to learn more about Steinbruck and his journal, I had many interesting conversations on the phone, on the Net, in libraries, coffee shops, bars, and bookshops, in Montreal, Toronto, Ottawa, Winnipeg, Vancouver, and Prince of Wales, with many strange and interesting creatures: amateur historians, greedy antiquarians, eccentric and secretive collectors, elitist curators and passionate "ordinary" Canadians enraptured by their country's history. Along the way I visited archives, apartments, and attics and was searched for sharp objects and stripped of and made to wear white gloves before I could touch the delicate parchments and paper pages of other fur traders' journals.

Something happened during this quest. I began a parallel journey, the journey that resulted in the writing of *In the Worshipful Company of Skinners*.

Looking through other fur traders' journals in McGill University's Rare Books and Special Collections Division, the McCord Museum, and the Hudson's Bay Company Archives in Manitoba for any mention of Steinbruck's presence, I became absorbed by their accounts. I started to copy out lines and events that struck my fancy because of their content and tone.

The content interested me because it was so ordinary and yet so extraordinary at the same time. The entries record mainly daily activities: trades, inventories, comings and goings, and encounters with strange and plentiful human and non-human creatures. It seems that every exchange, verbal or material, is duly noted. Alongside this obsessive accounting, the writers document their struggle to survive. And yet, though their world consisted of constant hardship, they did not consider their actions to be extraordinary or heroic. This was their daily life.

I was fascinated by the unfailing sameness of tone in these texts. As might be expected, the tone is flat in the accounts of trades, the recording of weather and location. But the content isn't limited to record keeping. There are sufficient entries describing excessive drinking and ensuing violence, deprivation and near-starvation, and life-or-death races, to merit a canoe-load of melodrama. These events, however, are recorded with the same flatness of emotion as the trading records. There is a strange sense of equal value allocated to all the journal entries. As a result, both the mundane and the extraordinary gain relevance and impact—the ordinary because of the exceptional, and the exceptional because of the ordinary. I started to think that there was poetry in these journals.

So I began stealing texts, selecting entries that I found striking. In the first version of what has become this book, I stayed true to the traders' words. At first, I simply broke them into lines so that the lines were complete phrases. However, as time and revisions came and went, I discovered that stealing texts and breaking lines were not enough. I needed more than just verbatim transcriptions with line breaks. I started to rework some of the traders' phrasings to suit the poems, trying to keep the spirit of their syntax, resonance, rhythms and musicality.

As I was working at these alterations, I contemplated the overall form and tone as well. I wanted each poem to have the feel of a trader's journal, if not its actual form. I played with a number of approaches. Most of the original journal entries are marked off by dates, but I didn't want that kind of timeline. I wanted the timeline to be composed of events and themes rather than dates. That is why I settled on a word or phrase as a hook for each poem. The repetition of these words or phrases at the beginning of stanzas is meant to signify the passage of time. This repetitive structure seems appropriate, because the original entries often have such a simple construct and rhythm. I also tried to capture the journals' factual nature, their flatness of tone, and their "listing" structure. I tried to let the "factual images" speak for themselves and in doing so, let the reader suggest a subtext. Finally, I created a character who is a composite of many traders. He starts out as a thirteen-year-old apprentice from the Orkney Islands who, as he crosses the country, gains experience and perhaps evolves by the time of his retirement. So even though these are found texts, they too have evolved into something more complex than just a record. They have evolved into a journal that is of the past and of the now.

Poems often lie to tell the truth. Poets manipulate language, imagery, lines, and rhythms to get to the heart of the matter. During the five years of visions and revisions of the phrasing, syntax and images, the poems in *In the Worshipful Company of Skinners* became a collage of the found, the manipulated, and the invented journal of Canada.

As I was rewriting and reforming the found texts into poems and writing brand-new ones, a theme began to emerge. Although different themes exist within the individual poems, I started to sense a larger one, the Canadian Identity. The search for this elusive goal is second only to finding the Northwest Passage (and now that we have done that, it might be our first goal, if we cared).

Individuals and nations often identify and value themselves and others by the labours they undertake. Another way we individually and collectively identify ourselves is through our creation myth(s). We explain ourselves to ourselves and to others via myths. A creation story roots us in a collective consciousness. In Canada we seem to have few of these myths. The story of how we made this country doesn't make for good myths, or so we think. I must clarify that when I talk about "we," I am talking about the Europeans. The Natives did not live in the New World, they lived on their land. They had their own creation myths, as weird and varied as the European ones. But those who came here did not need gods, demi-gods, romantic heroes, fantastic beasts, or great adventures with moral, social, cultural and collective significance. They were here to work hard and prosper. They came on behalf of absentee owners and boards of directors to exploit the new garden. And the motives of these traders, or employees, hardly seem heroic. Their grand ambition was to work for the Company, become partners in the Company, and become wealthy. They aspired to be rich, powerful, and comfortable bourgeois. These were practical ambitions, not unlike the aspirations of most Canadians today, and they required the security of a collective. I do not mean to imply that there were no outstanding, brave individuals among the traders, but on the whole, what drove them was the belief that their success and wealth lay with the enrichment of the Company and their desire to be a profitable part of it. This required an intricate and fascinating entwinement of self and the Company.

Trade is not usually viewed as a very noble, virtuous, heroic, or relevant topic for poetry. But the truth is that trade created this county. Trade is our creation myth. Our earliest creators are, for better or worse, the Companies; and our heroes are those who desired to belong to the bourgeosie. Canada was created by trade, for trade and of trade. It didn't emerge out of a once-upon-a-time or a battle between gods or wizards. It emerged from the daily trades and struggles among companies, "White Canadians," "Bois Brûlés," "Savages," the land, and the elements. And in the process the participants created the intricate and intertwined consciousness that we are, and are up against, today. In a sense, they made us all employers and emplyees of the worshipful company of skinners.

Endre Farkas
June 20, 2003
Vaudreuil-Dorion

Acknowledgements

I would like to thank my editor Catherine Hunter for her care in shaping this manuscript. Her comments, questions and commas were invaluable. As well, my thanks to Uli Mast, who knows much more than me about this subject, for sharing his deep passion for this time in Canadian history. And, finally, I want to thank the usual suspects who lent, ears and shoulders.